MAY 19 2006

W9-CKM-537

LEADERS OF THE
MIDDLE AGES™

HENRY VIII

The King, His Six Wives, and His Court

rosen
central™

The Rosen Publishing Group, Inc., New York

LEADERS OF THE MIDDLE AGES™

HENRY VIII — The King, His Six Wives, and His Court

Nick Ford

rosen central™

The Rosen Publishing Group, Inc., New York

To my father

Published in 2005 by The Rosen Publishing Group, Inc.
29 East 21st Street, New York, NY 10010

First Edition

Library of Congress Cataloging-in-Publication Data

Ford, Nick.
Henry VIII: The king, his six wives, and his court / by Nick Ford.
    p. cm. — (Leaders of the Middle Ages)
Includes bibliographical references and index.
Contents: The king who broke the mold—The young prince and his world—Young King Henry—His majesty's pleasure—Henry's crusade—Marriage problems—Rome, Reformation, and rebellion—Old King Henry—The legacy.
ISBN 1-4042-0163-7 (lib. bdg.)
1. Henry VIII, King of England, 1491–1547—Juvenile literature.
2. Great Britain—History—Henry VIII, 1509–1547—Juvenile literature.
3. Great Britain—Kings and rulers—Biography—Juvenile literature.
[1. Henry VIII, King of England, 1491–1547. 2. Great Britain—History—Henry VIII, 1509–1547. 3. Kings, queens, rulers, etc.]
I. Title: Henry the Eighth. II. Title. III. Series.
DA332.F67 2005
942.05'2'092—dc22

                                                          2003027161

Manufactured in the United States of America

On the cover: Henry VIII, king of England, shown in *The Field of the Cloth of Gold*, 1520

CONTENTS

LAND AT THE TIME OF HENRY VIII

SCOTLAND

IRELAND

WALES

ENGLAND

London

NETHERLANDS

Rotterdam

Cleves

Calais

Therouanne

Tournai

Boulogne

GERMANY

Paris

SWITZERLAND

FRANCE

ITALY

Rome

Aragon

SPAIN

MEDITERRANEAN SEA

SICILY

AFRICA

Introduction: The King Who Broke the Mold

King Henry VIII of England was a legend in his own lifetime. His dynamic but contradictory character has continued to fascinate people for five centuries. Today, no other medieval ruler is so easily recognizable. He is among the few that nearly everybody knows—not only by name, but by the things he did.

He dared to defy the pope, the ruler of Christendom, and make himself the head of his own church. He had six wives, in an age when this was unheard of. And he even ordered two of them to be executed! He successfully defended England against the biggest foreign invasion since 1066, when almost every ruler and country in Europe was against him. He designed warships and palaces. He led armies in battle and laid the foundations of what was to become the United Kingdom of Great Britain.

This portrait of King Henry VIII at age forty-five was painted by German-born Hans Holbein. In 1526, Holbein left Switzerland for England with a letter of recommendation from the great scholar Erasmus of Rotterdam. Erasmus had written to friends (one of whom was Sir Thomas More) recommending Holbein. Speaking of the state of art in England, Erasmus said, "The arts here are freezing." Once installed in England, Holbein was given the title of court painter by King Henry VIII. He painted many famous portraits of royals, including this one. Aside from painting, Holbein also produced a number of designs for items in gold. Holbein's portraits of King Henry are meant to impress the viewer and illustrate how powerful a ruler he was.

He was handsome, charming, clever, and courageous. However, he was capable of turning into an ugly, suspicious tyrant who was feared even by those closest to him. He had a great love of people. However, if someone crossed him, he would have them killed without hesitation. He was very strong-willed, yet he seems to have been manipulated by others. He loved tradition but was never afraid to destroy the old and build something new in its place. Although he was a great athlete and soldier, he sometimes behaved cowardly in his personal relationships. Oddly enough, as strong and powerful as he was, he became desperately afraid of disease and old age. He was a sensitive musician who wrote many beautiful songs and poems, yet he could order executions by the hundreds.

Ever since William Shakespeare made him the hero of a play half a century after his death, Henry VIII has been the subject of more books and movies than any other English king or queen. So colorful and complex were the man and the times he shaped, there is always something new to discover and say about him.

History has many famous heroes and villains who will long be remembered. However, it is hard to find Henry's equal among them—for he was both. He was England's last medieval king and its first modern ruler.

THE YOUNG PRINCE AND HIS WORLD

Prince Henry Tudor was born in Greenwich Palace, near London, on June 28, 1491. His elder brother, Arthur, Prince of Wales, was then five years old. His eldest sister, Margaret, was two. Mary, the youngest, was born five years later. There had also been another, older sister, Elizabeth. However, she died at age three, and a second brother, Edmund, lived only eighteen months. At that time, it was common for children to die young.

By the time he was two years old, Henry was constable of Dover Castle and warden of the Cinque Ports. At age three, he was made a knight, when he had to ride a great warhorse in a procession to Westminster Abbey in London. Soon after, he was also made Duke of York. It may seem silly that a very young child should be given responsibilities like these, but there were good reasons for doing so. His father, King Henry VII, knew that money was power. He believed that a king who needed money would be controlled by those he borrowed from. Important officials who governed large castles or ran the seaports, which provided ships for England's defense, earned high wages. But by giving these jobs to his children, the king was able to keep the wages for himself. Instead, he would hire lower-paid, lower-ranking deputies, who were answerable directly to him.

BEING THE SON OF A KING

When Henry grew older, he would begin to learn the business of government like his brother Arthur, who was ruling Wales by age ten. The king appointed trusted advisers for the young prince. But as he grew more experienced, he took on the full responsibilities of his rank. In medieval Europe, this was quite normal. As soon as children were old enough, they were taught how to help with their parents' work, and the sooner they learned, the better. Royalty was no exception. Responsibility came at a very early age, often because most people did not live as long as they do today.

There was one other reason why Henry was made Duke of York. Until 1485, only six years before

This oil portrait of Henry VII is by an unknown artist. Painted in 1505, it is the oldest painting in the National Portrait Gallery in London. Henry VII was the son of Edmund Tudor, and he took the throne of England after defeating Richard III at the Battle of Bosworth Field in 1485. He was the first of five Tudor monarchs.

his birth, a long and bloody civil war had been fought between two groups of aristocratic families and their followers, the Yorkists and the Lancastrians.

Both claimed the right by ancestry to rule England. The Tudors belonged to the House (or family group) of Lancaster. Henry's father had defeated and killed the last Yorkist king (Richard the III), married Princess Elizabeth of York, and established a firm grip on the kingdom. However, there were still survivors of the House of York (or people who claimed to be) who were plotting to seize the throne by armed rebellion. One rebellion was led by someone who said he was the last Duke of York. However, he had last been seen ten years before, and many thought he had been murdered. Henry VII made young Henry Duke of York in order to show that only the king had the right to give or take away titles as he wished.

DAILY LIFE FOR YOUNG HENRY

Young Henry had his own group of servants, including a band of minstrels and a jester. He also had his own tutors, including a poet named John Skelton. Skelton taught Henry Latin and Greek as well as how to write songs and play them on the lute. Henry loved music and singing and became quite an inspired musician and composer.

Henry's childhood was spent mostly at Eltham Palace in Kent, near London. As it did for most people, Henry's day began at dawn. This was done in order to make the most of the daylight. Having washed and dressed, he had to attend matins, or morning prayer, which was conducted by his own chaplain. He then joined the rest of the household for Mass at 6 AM. Afterward, he would eat a light breakfast—usually bread with meat or cheese and a little watered wine or weak beer (beer was usual for everyone). By 6:30 AM, his lessons would start. These included reading, writing, French, Latin, Greek, mathematics, law, philosophy, geography, and history—especially history

FRIENDS AND SCHOOLMATES

Henry did not study alone. He was often joined by cousins such as the Courtnays (the sons of the Earl of Devon), who lived nearby. Edward Pallet, an orphan who had been adopted by Henry's mother, the queen, and who lived in the royal household, accompanied him. And they were joined by William Compton, Henry's page, who would become his lifelong friend.

Also in the group was Henry's best friend, Charles Brandon. Charles's grandfather William had been Henry VII's standard-bearer and was killed at the Battle of Bosworth. It was at this battle that Henry's father won the crown of England. The Yorkist king Richard III had charged at Henry's father to kill him with his battle-ax, but William Brandon had defended him with his own life. From that point on, the Brandon family enjoyed special royal favor, and the two boys, Henry and Charles, grew up together and were friends for life.

Charles Brandon was not as smart as Henry but he was older, bigger, and stronger. Henry looked up to him like an elder brother. At first, Charles could outride, outrun, and out-fight Henry. However, Henry trained so hard that by the time both were teenagers, Henry was frequently the winner. Until his late middle age, Henry kept up the well-deserved reputation for being an athlete and a fighter who was almost impossible to beat.

of his royal ancestors. This was especially important because both Henry's father's and his mother's forefathers had been kings.

By 10 AM—halfway through the day—it was time for the midday meal. Also present would be a tutor to supervise table manners. The tutor would hit Henry with a stick if he misbehaved. This harsh punishment was seen as necessary. It was believed that children destined to control others when they grow up must first learn to control themselves—especially in public.

The afternoons were devoted to sports and martial arts—jousting on horseback, practice fighting with blunted weapons, and archery. There were handguns in those days, but as they were relatively new inventions, they were unreliable and not thought of as being suitable weapons for a young gentleman. To help him grow strong and fit for these warlike exercises (which often included wearing a full suit of armor), Henry would run races, wrestle,

This is a French illuminated manuscript from 1470 featuring a scene from a tournament. This illustration is from the chivalric romance called *Le Petit Jean de Saintre*.

leap ditches, and climb walls with other boys of the household.

At about 4 PM, the household would gather in the palace chapel for vespers. This was followed by another light meal—supper—and in the early evening, the boys of the royal household would join the girls. They would then sing, dance, and play musical instruments, especially the lute. Games of chess, checkers, and backgammon followed, and the children were allowed to gamble with small amounts of money. Gambling was regarded as being as much a social accomplishment as music or dancing. At the time, it was unusual to play games without betting on them. (The usual word for gambling was "gaming.") Then about 9 PM, it was time for bed.

LIFE IN THE PUBLIC EYE

Young Henry grew up without his brother. By the time they were old enough to be good company for each other, Prince Arthur, who was heir to the throne of England and Prince of Wales, had already been sent away to rule Wales as his father's deputy. They saw each other only at ceremonial events or when the family spent Christmas together. On these rare occasions, Henry, Arthur, and their sisters would go hunting with their father. All the children learned riding, hawking, and shooting deer with a longbow. Hunting would become a lifelong passion for Henry.

The royal children were an important part of public occasions, and a great deal of royal life was lived in the public eye. Even on ordinary days, the king had hundreds of guests at dinner. Because of this, beginning at an early age, Henry had to behave

This 1523 Hans Holbein painting of Erasmus hangs in the Musée du Louvre in Paris. Erasmus was a great scholar who studied the text of the Greek New Testament. He published a corrected Greek text that became important in England during the Reformation. Erasmus, whose full name was Desiderius Erasmus, was born in 1466 in Rotterdam. He died in 1536.

with the dignity and authority of the rank into which he had been born.

When Henry was eight, the famous scholar Erasmus of Rotterdam visited the court. As noted in Carolly Erickson's book *Great Harry: A Life of King Henry VIII*, Erasmus wrote to a friend that Prince Henry showed "already something of royalty in his demeanor [attitude], in which there was a certain dignity combined with a singular courtesy."

A ROYAL WEDDING

At age ten, Henry was given an important task. Prince Arthur was to be married to the king of Spain's daughter, Princess Katherine of Aragon. Since Spanish custom demanded that the bride and groom should not see each other before the wedding, Henry had to take his brother's place. He had the job of meeting the princess and her royal retinue when they arrived in England. Then he had to escort them to London. Henry could not speak Spanish, and Katherine did not understand English, so they probably spoke to each other in Latin.

During the ten days of festivities that followed the royal wedding, it was not Arthur whom everyone noticed, but Henry. Partnered with his sister Margaret (then age twelve), he danced so well that everyone applauded and asked them to dance again. Overheated, Henry threw off his heavy formal gown (a thing never done in polite society) and danced better than before, to even more applause.

Henry had enjoyed being at the center of attention at court. Little did he know that soon he would spend a great deal of time in the public eye. Nor could he have known that the dignified, sixteen-year-old Spanish princess he had escorted to his brother's wedding would one day be so important in his life.

YOUNG KING HENRY

In April 1502, only five months after his marriage to Katherine of Aragon, Arthur suddenly fell ill of a fever and died. The marriage had been a political alliance with Spain against France, and Princess Katherine's dowry (which Henry VII was eager to collect) was a small fortune. The obvious solution to both the prince's and the princess's parents seemed that Katherine should now marry Prince Henry.

DIFFICULT TIMES

According to the rules of the Catholic Church, before a man could marry his brother's wife, he had to get special permission from the pope. Seeing as Katherine had not become pregnant during their short marriage, Henry was regarded as next in line to the throne. While waiting for word from the pope,

This portrait of Katherine of Aragon was painted around 1530 by an unknown artist. Katherine was the youngest child of Ferdinand and Isabella of Spain. In the portrait, Katherine is wearing an English hood. At the time, married women were supposed to cover their heads in public. Wealthy and fashionable women had a wider selection of head wear than did poorer women.

Henry was given the title of Prince of Wales, along with a huge set of new responsibilities. His father and Katherine argued endlessly over the delayed payment of the dowry. It was not a happy year for the family.

The next year was even worse. Henry's mother died after giving birth to a baby girl, who also died soon after. King Henry VII was so sad that he shut himself away in his bedchamber. He would not come out or speak to anyone for days. In the year following his tenth birthday, Prince Henry had lost his older brother, his mother, and his youngest sister. Meanwhile, his favorite sister, Margaret, then

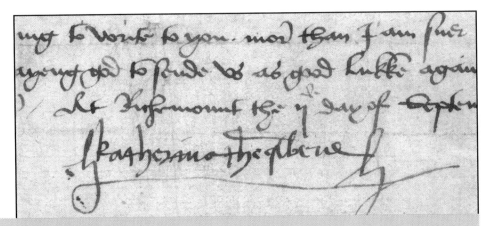

This is Katherine of Aragon's signature. It reads "Katherine the Quene [Queen]."

fourteen, had been sent far away to Scotland to marry their king, James IV. The following Christmas must have been very miserable.

However, there was little time for the young prince to feel sorry for himself. Once his father had recovered from the shock of the queen's death, he decided to take charge of Henry and train him personally for the day he would be king.

KING HENRY VII

Henry's father was both a good and a bad example of rulership: Henry VII made the English monarchy powerful and dignified. His new palace at Richmond was spectacular. It made a wonderful stage for theatrical ceremonies that left people in awe. The king presided over law and order at home and a sense of peace abroad that England had not seen for generations. The royal treasury was overflowing at a time when most monarchs lived in permanent debt. England was fast becoming a nation of importance in Europe. English expeditions led by John Cabot had been launched to the New World. They were the first to map the eastern coast of North America from Labrador to Virginia. Their discoveries rivaled Christopher Columbus's discoveries of Cuba and the Gulf of Mexico.

However, Henry VII's reign was drawing to a close. The father with whom Henry (age eleven) now came into close daily contact with was growing old and ill—physically and mentally. He was becoming obsessed with getting money and treasure. Many people thought he was a miser (a cheapskate), though they were too afraid to say so openly. He spent a lot of time and money on schemes for turning other metals into gold by alchemy. As well, he obsessively collected holy relics, with which he surrounded himself constantly. Even during medieval times, this behavior seemed superstitious to the point of madness.

The old king's temper became very unpredictable, and his moods became violent. Once he suddenly grew so angry with Henry that for no apparent reason he fiercely attacked him as though he would kill him.

It seemed that young Henry's teacher in kingship could no longer tell the difference between using power for the good of the nation and abusing power to satisfy his personal desires.

HENRY THE TEENAGER

Meanwhile, Henry was growing into a tall, handsome, powerfully built young man who people said resembled his grandfather, Edward IV. Edward IV's strong physique, good looks, charm, and skill as a knight had made him enormously popular. The less like a child and the more like a man Henry became, the more his father seemed to dislike him. He kept him hard at work, confined to a room next to his own. Here, he was surrounded by guards and was rarely allowed to see his few friends. His only release from this daily ordeal was physical exercise—fencing, wrestling, riding, and hunting—for which he was grudgingly allowed outdoors. However, he was never allowed beyond the palace grounds or out of sight of the bodyguards who followed him everywhere. The king was probably concerned for his son's safety and the stability of the kingdom. But for young Henry, it must have felt like being under arrest. In 1508, when he was sixteen, a visiting ambassador noticed that the

This is an image of Henry VIII jousting before Katherine of Aragon to celebrate the birth of their son, Henry, in 1511. Unfortunately, young Henry did not live for long. Here, Henry VIII is demonstrating his strength and agility in a jousting tournament. The skills developed by a knight in tournaments were good training for the battlefield.

prince was so withdrawn he would not even speak to his father unless he was asked a direct question.

Despite the fact that he had promised King Ferdinand of Spain that young Henry would marry Princess Katherine as soon as he was fourteen, King Henry VII refused to allow him to marry her. King Ferdinand therefore refused to pay King Henry the balance of her dowry. Out of spite, Henry's father forbade Katherine to go home to Spain, would not allow her to appear at court, and refused to give her any money to live on. She had hardly any visitors, and life must have been hard for her. Nonetheless, she never gave up hope that one day she would marry Prince Henry and be his queen.

A YOUNG KING

At long last, on April 21, 1509, the old king died. Within seven weeks, just before his seventeenth birthday, Henry—now King Henry VIII—married Princess Katherine at Greenwich. A few days later, on Midsummer Day, they were crowned king and queen in Westminster Abbey. As king, Henry was determined that things would be different.

The old king's advisers, now members of Henry's Privy Council, must have found the change very difficult. Henry wanted all his friends around him. After six years of being under his father's strict personal supervision, he wanted to enjoy himself. Two advisers—both elderly bishops—wrote to King Ferdinand, asking him to persuade his son-in-law to take his new responsibilities more seriously. However, it was not surprising that after being dominated by his father for so long, a strong, energetic, high-spirited youth of seventeen would want some freedom from serious-minded old men. These councillors he inherited from his father were still following the old king's orders. This was because Henry would not become a legal adult and—thus, able to rule by himself—until his twenty-first birthday.

KING HENRY RIDES OUT

Ever since Arthur's death, when he became the only male heir to the throne, Henry had not been allowed to take part in jousting. However, one day in January 1510, he heard that some of the courtiers were planning a tournament in secret. It was kept a secret because they knew that Henry's advisers would not be pleased if they found out. Henry and his page, Will Compton, dressed in plain armor so that no one would recognize them. They arrived for the jousting uninvited and unannounced, as two mysterious strangers. Fighting as a team, they won nearly every combat until Will was severely wounded. When Henry went to help him, someone recognized him and shouted, "God save the king!" Henry took off his helmet and showed himself to the cheering crowd.

Henry was growing confident enough to begin to take charge. He took part in every tournament and announced that, outside the hunting season, many more jousts were to be held. He had good reasons for doing this, other than for his own enjoyment. It meant that young, untrustworthy, ambitious noblemen would be where he could watch them closely. As well, they would become fit and

An image of Henry VIII's armor, circa 1540. This is an example of tournament armor, which was designed to protect all parts of the body. The armor had hinges to allow the wearer to move. The armor was either padded or worn over padding—both of which added a great deal of bulk and weight to the wearer. During medieval times, armor was extremely valuable. Onlookers could tell the wealth of the wearer by his armor. At the time, the cost of a suit of armor was about the same as the price of a car today. The armor shown here would be the equivalent of a Rolls Royce.

would gain expertise in the arts of war. As a young boy, Henry had read the histories of his ancestors and their victories over England's traditional enemy, France. He dreamed of doing the same.

The young noblemen of the court must have found the death of the old king a welcome change. Men of learning saw in Henry a young man who was not only an athlete but also someone whose natural intelligence and excellent education had made him a very good scholar. Henry's father had employed brilliant academics to reflect highly on the king and the kingdom, but Henry aspired to be one himself. "Without knowledge," he said to a courtier, Lord Mountjoy, who passed his words on to Erasmus in a letter, "life would not be worth our having." Remembering the visit from Erasmus (one of the best minds in Europe) when he was eight, Henry wrote to him often. Henry invited Erasmus to come and live in England.

About the time that Henry went jousting in disguise, Queen Katherine was about to give birth to their first child—a baby girl. Unfortunately, she was born dead. Katherine soon became pregnant again, and on New Year's Day 1511, she gave birth to a son. Henry was delighted. The arrival of a male heir (christened Henry) to the kingdom was celebrated with pageants, tournaments, banquets, and services of thanksgiving. The cost of all of this would be more than a billion dollars. Sadly, in two months, the child was dead. Henry may have begun to wonder whether this was a sign that God was angry with him for some reason. It became a doubt that would grow to a certainty in his mind in the years to come.

His majesty's pleasure

Henry worked hard and played hard, and he expected everyone around him to do the same. He loved people, and he needed to be loved and admired in return. This was not just part of his personality but part of the secret of being a successful monarch.

The many descriptions that exist of Henry VIII—from letters written by courtiers and officials, ambassadors, and visiting foreign merchants—were not just written by flatterers looking for favors. Though they may not have liked him, even visiting representatives of hostile foreign countries and political enemies at home certainly could not help admiring him.

THE COURT

The court was not a particular place in a palace. It existed wherever the king happened to be. Henry had several royal

This 1519 painting is by Lambert Bertrand. In it, Bishop Sherborne, of Sherborne Abbey in Dorset in western England, is asking King Henry to confirm a charter (or an agreement) between the abbey and the king, which Henry wrote in 1519.

palaces, mostly in or near London. Each could house hundreds of servants and guests under one roof. It was often necessary to move out for a while to allow the palace to be thoroughly cleaned.

It was important for the king to be seen throughout his kingdom. He had to keep an eye on all his subjects (especially the powerful nobles) and to maintain his popularity. He would sometimes plan a tour, called a royal progress, where he would invite himself to stay at noblemen's great houses and castles along the route. This also saved him a great deal of money. By 1513, after only four years as king, he had spent all the money his father had left him in the royal treasury. It was very expensive for noblemen to provide the king and all his followers with hospitality, even for a few days. However, it was an honor that could not be refused.

When the king traveled, he was accompanied by a great retinue of courtiers, friends, officials, servants, and soldiers—along with all their horses. They needed to be housed, fed, and suitably entertained. Henry would also bring along his own furniture, gold and silver vessels for eating and drinking, and other household items. This even included his four-poster bed with curtains (this was a security measure because poisoned blades could be hidden in mattresses). As well, he had his own locksmith change the locks of his private quarters. Along with his musicians and other entertainers, these processions must have been quite a spectacle. Towns through which the royal progress passed would often stage a pageant to welcome him.

BETTING AND GAMBLING

Henry was a generous man. He loved gambling, and in those days, bets were made at cards, dice, board games, horse racing, tournaments, wrestling matches, archery contests—practically anything. A well-bred aristocrat was expected to be able to bet and lose huge sums of money without seeming to worry. And of course, Henry was expected to lose great sums of money more cheerfully than anybody else. His personal accounts often show daily losses of hundreds of pounds—perhaps as much as half a million dollars at a time.

To the medieval mind, gambling was not regarded as sinful (unless you cheated, and there were plenty of professional gamblers who made a dangerous living that way). The real sin was having a reputation for

The Malmesbury/Caird Cup, dating from 1529, was made in London. This silver cup is an important example of early English silver from the reign of King Henry VIII. The cup, which is made from seven separate sections, had not been noticed until 1950, when Arthur Grimwade discovered it in the collection of the Earl of Malmesbury.

being too careful about money, as Henry's father had been. One of the virtues of a medieval prince was called magnificence, which meant extravagant generosity.

MUSIC AND MASQUERADE

Henry founded what he called the King's Musick, an academy of singers and musicians—the best that money could buy anywhere. He more than doubled the number of his father's court musicians, who had been used only for ceremonial and public occasions. Their job was now to be wherever Henry was, whenever he wanted music. Many of these musicians were composers in their own right. The King's Musick, together with the choir of the Chapel Royal, became famous throughout Europe. They set a standard for the courts of other monarchs. Expert performers and composers even came from Italy (which was generally regarded as the center of sophisticated culture) in the hope of getting a royal audition. One musician even committed suicide when the king did not hire him.

On more private occasions, such as small parties at which only friends were present, Henry would give performances on a variety of woodwind, stringed, and keyboard instruments, including organs. Henry

This is a page from the fifteenth-century manuscript *Livre de Messire Lancelot du Lac.* It illustrates the legend of King Arthur. In this image, the Holy Grail appears to the knights of the Round Table.

took a great interest in designing and improving these instruments. Some of Henry's compositions are thought to be so good that they are still played and sung today. The best known is "Greensleeves."

No festive occasion was complete without a masque. This was a combination of theater, singing, dance, and often stage combat, combined with movable three-dimensional scenery and special effects.

einmanibrance los hons qui ampres too
ce facordent rour si entrient en lacure. et
aunes de telr en peut pour souster plus
tr en peut qui ne prudr̃ent fors quelcurs
er leurs efats. Car moue se soient en les
us plusieurs. et le roy qui cout ce ce esuoi

Poets such as John Skelton wrote these masques, but Henry probably suggested the subjects or ideas. These not only enhanced pageants and processions but also provided spectacular entertainment for large, formal dinners at court.

During these occasions, the doors of the great dining hall would open and costumed actors, musicians, and scenery on wheels would come in. Sometimes, this was accompanied by live animals or special effects such as fireworks.

Those who took part were often disguised as ancient heroes and heroines, gods and goddesses, giants, and monsters from Greek and Roman mythology. Sometimes, they would be characters from British fairy tales and legends, such as those of Robin Hood or King Arthur. Henry liked to take part himself, especially since people were not supposed to know who he was under the disguise. He liked to be applauded for his performance—and not because he was the king.

Henry had a cousin, Edward Neville, who was the same age and very like Henry in appearance. Often they would change clothes and places so that the king would appear to be watching the proceedings, while in fact he was among the performers. In this way, he would sometimes make fun of important visiting foreign dignitaries. This not only appealed to Henry's love of practical jokes, but it must have also given him a sense of freedom. In this way, he could escape the responsibilities and restraints of being the king for a while. It also meant that he could hear the court gossip and learn firsthand what was being said about him and others of the court.

THE PLEASURES OF LEARNING

Henry enjoyed the pursuit of knowledge as much as he enjoyed masquerades and hunting. According to Erickson's *Great Harry: A Life of King Henry VIII*, Thomas More, a scholar and royal official, as well as the king's friend, once wrote to his friend Erasmus, "Our sovereign [king] has himself more learning than any English monarch ever possessed before him." Henry's library at Greenwich had more than 300 books. This was considered a huge number for any collection at the time. This is because at the time, most books were still written by hand, a process that was very time-consuming.

Just as he liked to organize jousts, Henry arranged debates on philosophy and religion. He enjoyed these combats of the mind as much as the contests in the tiltyard. In these mental battles, Queen Katherine, who was a well-educated intellectual, was able to join her husband as an equal. Like Henry and the group of scholars at the court, such as More and Erasmus, Katherine was involved in the "new learning." This was an educational movement based on the study of newly rediscovered original Greek works on science, religion, and philosophy, instead of poor copies in medieval Latin.

On one occasion, Katherine even outsmarted Erasmus, who had made a new Latin translation of the Bible from many ancient Greek texts. Conservative scholars believed that this would lead to heresy. They wondered how anyone could dare to think he could improve upon the Latin Bible that Saint Jerome himself had translated from the Greek a thousand years earlier? Katherine asked him why, if Saint Jerome was in heaven, Erasmus thought he could do better. Was Erasmus wiser than the saint? Erasmus was stuck for an answer. Later, and rather grudgingly, he admitted that Katherine was (as noted in *Great Harry: A Life of King Henry VIII*) "miraculously learned for a woman." Henry probably laughed at that. After all, he was fond of women with lively minds.

Henry's Crusade

CHAPTER 4

In 1511, Henry had his first chance to prove himself to be a chivalric soldier-king like his ancestors. The French king, Louis XII, had cornered the pope's army in northern Italy and was planning to overthrow him and force the election of a new pope who would favor French interests. Pope Julius II responded by calling for a "Holy League" of nations to defend the church and drive the French from Italy. It was to be a crusade. Henry was quick to join and set about raising and equipping an invasion force.

It took nearly two years. This was because the old king Henry VII had spent very little on warships and other military equipment. Instead, he preferred to outwit his enemies with diplomacy. But young King Henry VIII spent his father's compiled wealth freely, and by 1513, his new army and navy were ready.

Julius II *(above)* was pope from 1503 to 1513. After him came Pope Leo X (1513–1521). Julius II had granted a special dispensation that allowed Henry to marry the widow of his dead brother Arthur. At this time, there were very detailed rules about whom people could marry. If two individuals were considered to be too closely related, the marriage was not allowed.

The pope told Henry that, if they won, he would support his ancestral claim to be king of France. Since the civil war between Lancaster and York in 1455 to 1485, England's dominions in France had shrunk to a few miles of territory around the seaport of Calais (the part of France closest to the English coast). This made a good foot-hold from which Henry could invade and (he hoped) reconquer all the lands his great-great-uncle Henry V had won a century before.

ARMIES AND ARMS

Henry had bought thousands of the new handguns, but his troops still mainly relied on longbows. His chancellor, the fabulously rich Cardinal Thomas Wolsey, had purchased a set of twelve huge siege cannons nicknamed the Twelve Apostles. These were designed to smash (at long range) the thick stone walls of French fortresses and cities (while terrifying the defenders). Each one hurled a cannonball weighing 260 pounds (118 kilograms) and needed twenty-four heavy draft horses or oxen to pull it. Henry had also commissioned twenty-four smaller cannons called curtolds. These fired 60-pound (27 kg) balls and needed a dozen horses each to pull them.

The allies of the Holy League each planned to attack France from different directions—the pope and his Italian army from the southeast, King Ferdinand of Spain from the southwest, Emperor Maximilian from Germany in the east, and Henry's English army from the north.

The English invasion fleet fought off French attempts to stop it from landing at Calais, and Henry was soon ready to march into France at the head of his army. With him were his old childhood friends. Charles Brandon was second in command. Henry's page and jousting companion, Will Compton, had a command of his own. And Cardinal Wolsey commanded his own troops as well as the battery of siege cannons he had presented to Henry.

Henry was optimistic, but his allies let him down. Ferdinand suddenly changed his mind and refused to move out of Spain. Meanwhile, Pope Julius had died, and his successor, Leo X, hesitated to carry out the plan. This meant that only Emperor Maximilian sent an army to join up with Henry's. When it arrived, it was only half the size that had been promised, and even then, Maximilian asked Henry to pay his soldiers, saying he was very short of money.

It seemed that of all the leaders of the Holy League, only Henry believed in keeping his promises. However, he was also the only ruler who could afford a long and expensive war. Because he was inexperienced, however his allies did not take him seriously. Henry was furious and vowed that England would fight France without their help—and win.

Another setback followed. While Henry's army was besieging the key city of Thérouanne, news arrived that King James VI of Scotland had declared war on England. Henry sent word to Queen Katherine, who was ruling England in his absence, to send the Earl of Surrey, Sir Thomas Howard, with a small army to meet the Scottish invasion while he concentrated on winning the war in France.

The French army, approaching Thérouanne, was outmaneuvered at nearby Guinegate. As the two armies met, about 1,100 English knights charged 2,000 French knights and scattered them. Henry joined in the pursuit against his councillors' advice. Because he was so impatient for glory, he let his cavalry run too far ahead of the main army and they had to turn back unsupported. Otherwise, Henry might have beaten the whole French army and become king of France. However, even in this relatively small fight, nine French standards were taken. And more than a hundred French noblemen were captured for ransom, as well as a great deal of arms and equipment. The French army was demoralized and was afraid to attack the English army again.

A MILITARY SUCCESS

In the end, the cities of Thérouanne, Lille, and Tournai were captured, along with five other fortified towns. The campaign was a success, and Henry, age twenty-one, had proved himself a leader to be taken seriously. However, the war had cost him one million pounds—almost all the wealth his father had left him. This shortage of money was to create problems for Henry during the rest of his reign.

While Henry was in France, the Scottish invasion had been crushed by the Earl of Surrey, Sir Thomas

Howard. The 40,000-strong Scottish army—led by King James—was defeated in just three hours by an English army half its size. Eleven thousand Scotsmen, including King James and most of his knights and nobles, were killed. The English lost only 1,500. Henry, who was delighted, rewarded the earl by making him the Duke of Norfolk and thus the highest-ranking nobleman in the kingdom. It was a wonderful year for Henry, who must have felt that at last his ambitions of becoming a victorious warrior-king were finally being realized.

Marriage Problems

In 1527, when Henry was thirty-six, something happened that would transform the whole character of his reign and change England forever. For all his love of show and pleasure, Henry was a deeply religious man. He believed that God's will on earth was made known through the Holy Catholic Church, which all people had to obey as a matter of sacred duty. It was also the duty of the king to see that all obeyed.

CHAPTER 5

KINGLY DUTIES

However, for Henry, two other duties were coming into conflict. The first was the duty of marriage. He had always said that he would have freely chosen to marry Queen Katherine, whatever the circumstances. Yet after seventeen years, she had given birth to three sons, none of whom survived more than a few weeks, and only one surviving daughter, Mary. Not only was Katherine growing too old to have any more children, but she was also becoming physically unattractive to Henry. He could not love a woman for her mind alone.

The second duty was for Henry to leave behind a son and, hence, an heir to the throne. This was necessary to ensure the stability and well-being of the kingdom. As it was, there were other candidates for the throne. These were descendants from the House of York, and without a clear succession, there could be great danger of civil war.

What troubled Henry was that for some years, he worried that he had no surviving male offspring because God was punishing him. Henry suspected that God was against him for disobeying the instruction in the Bible that stated, "If a man shall take his brother's wife, it is an impurity . . . they shall be childless." Even though the pope (God's chief representative on earth) had given permission for Henry to marry Katherine after his brother Arthur died, it seemed to Henry that perhaps not even the pope could say something was allowed when the Bible clearly stated that it was not.

After deep discussions with his religious advisers, Henry asked his chief minister, Cardinal Wolsey, to go to the pope and request an annulment—something only the pope could grant. But the pope was unwilling to reverse a papal decision. He also feared the anger of Charles V, King Ferdinand's grandson, who was now both king of Spain and the emperor of Austria (as well as being Queen Katherine's nephew).

In those days, it was not unusual for a powerful ruler to invade Rome with an army and depose (or kick out) a pope who displeased him. This forced the cardinals to elect another pope who would do what he wanted.

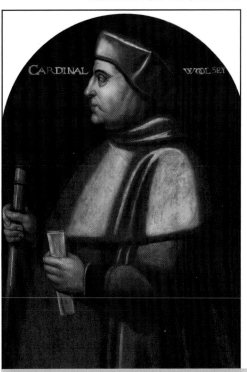

CARDINAL WOLSEY

This is a painting of Cardinal Thomas Wolsey (1475–1530) by an unknown artist. It dates from the late sixteenth century. Though he was a man of humble origins, his administrative skills soon made him the most important man in England after the king. However, his rapid rise to wealth made him unpopular with nobles and commoners.

QUEST FOR A MALE HEIR

Since 1524, Henry and Katherine had not shared a bed, though they appeared together in public.

Relations between them had become strained ever since the death of their first baby son in 1510. Henry had sought consolation in an affair with a highborn married lady of the court. However, Katherine had found out, despite Henry's efforts to keep it a secret. After that, Henry had other affairs. In 1518, Elizabeth Blount, one of the most beautiful ladies at court, became Henry's mistress and bore him a fine, healthy son. He was named Henry Fitzroy (which means "the king's son" in Old French), and Henry made him Duke of Richmond and Somerset.

Henry believed that if he could father healthy sons with other women, it was obviously due to some problem with Katherine that they could not produce a male heir together. Henry thought again about the curse in the Bible on a marriage with a dead brother's widow. He decided it was clearly his duty to marry again, regardless of what the pope said.

HENRY, ANNE BOLEYN, AND CARDINAL WOLSEY

In 1527, Henry fell in love with another court beauty, the Duke of Norfolk's granddaughter Anne Boleyn. He sent her expensive presents, and they exchanged love letters, many of which survive to this day.

The Boleyns were merchants who had become rich enough to marry into the old aristocracy, which had been depleted by the civil war. Like many other such families at that time, these "new men," as the aristocratic old families sneeringly called them, were highly ambitious. The road to unlimited power was to marry into the royal family. However, the

This portrait of Anne Boleyn was painted in the late sixteenth century. It was copied from an original that was made during her lifetime.

higher the climb, the more dangerous the fall.

Anne's family had made enemies with Cardinal Wolsey. He was a man of humble beginnings, who had risen through church and court offices to become the richest and most powerful man in England, aside from the king. The Boleyns wanted two things—to see their daughter Anne become queen and to see Wolsey destroyed.

Wolsey had many other enemies as well. In England, he was the deputy of both the king and pope.

His success made many people jealous, and his power and arrogance made many hate and fear him. However, Wolsey was not concerned. He felt that he need not worry about being unpopular or having enemies at court as long as the king could not manage without him.

Anne also hated Wolsey. He had prevented her from marrying Henry Percy, the man she loved. Percy was the heir to the Earl of Northumberland. The cardinal had already arranged a political marriage for Percy to the daughter of another nobleman. Wolsey had Anne banished from the court to her father's castle for three years. She swore that one day she would get even.

Henry wanted to make Anne his mistress, but she said she would only be his if they were married. Wolsey worked hard, presenting Henry's case for an annulment to the pope for more than a year, but with no success. He was in a difficult position. If he failed, Henry would be furious with him, but if he succeeded, one of his greatest enemies would become the new queen. If the case dragged on without a judgment, Henry would still need Wolsey and he would be safe from his enemies. Henry later accused Wolsey of deliberately delaying a judgment for this very reason.

COURT OF INQUIRY

The following year, in 1528, the pope sent Cardinal Lorenzo Campeggio from Rome to England to hold a court of inquiry, at which both the king and the queen gave evidence. Queen Katherine swore that Prince Arthur had not had sexual relations with her while they were married. This meant that her marriage to Arthur had never been legally valid.

She and her supporters also argued that there was another text in the Bible that said that a man must marry his dead brother's wife if they had no children. But Campeggio would not reach a decision. He did not want to risk angering the pope and Emperor Charles by deciding in Henry's favor. (Charles, the Holy Roman Emperor, was ruler of half of Europe and Katherine of Aragon's nephew.) Also, Campeggio did not dare decide against Henry for fear of what Henry might do to him while he was still in England. If an emperor could put a pope in prison, then a king could imprison a cardinal.

By 1529, Wolsey had run out of time. He had failed his master the king, and his enemies—especially Anne—wanted revenge. They persuaded Henry that Wolsey's widespread unpopularity as the king's chief minister reflected badly on him. This, coupled with

Henry's personal disappointment at Wolsey's failure to win an annulment, was enough for Henry to strip him of all wealth and royal offices. Wolsey was banished from court, and Henry gave his highest royal office—that of chancellor, or the king's chief legal adviser—to his friend Sir Thomas More. Wolsey died a broken man weeks later.

Campeggio suspended the court of inquiry and left England for Rome. Three more years of negotiations with the papal court in Rome came to nothing. Henry was now forty-two and badly needed a legal son and heir. He was impatient to marry Anne, with whom he seemed to have been madly in love. He decided that there was no more time to waste. He made Katherine retire to a royal manor far away from court, and in 1533, he secretly married Anne. Henry felt that once he presented the world with his new marriage, people who mattered could be brought around to see things his way.

SCANDAL

Henry was mistaken. The marriage was not popular. The coronation ceremony was spectacular, but the crowds who came to watch the procession pass

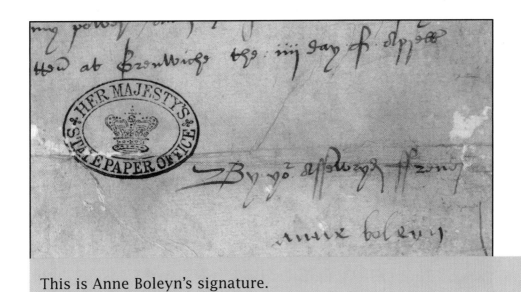

This is Anne Boleyn's signature.

through the streets of London were unenthusiastic, if not downright hostile.

Anne was only the daughter of a knight (although quite rich). For a commoner to be queen was almost unheard of. And for a king to put away his reigning queen and lawful wife against her will and against the church was absolutely scandalous. Most shocking of all was that, at the ceremony, people could see that Anne was very obviously pregnant. And she wore Queen Katherine's jewels in public for everyone to see.

Anne quickly became just as unpopular as Wolsey had been, for many of the same reasons. The common people felt jealous that a commoner had been raised so high by the king. Meanwhile, the aristocrats thought it was against the natural order of things. Both Wolsey and Anne had behaved arrogantly to powerful people they should have tried to befriend. The king's friendship and favor alone were not enough to protect anyone from enemies at court.

The pope ordered that Henry send Anne away from court and take Katherine back as his queen or face banishment from the Catholic Church. This meant that when Henry died, he would go to hell. However, Henry would not change his mind. He was convinced that he was in the right because God had showed that his marriage to Katherine was wrong. And he believed the pope opposed him for political, not religious, reasons. After he sent Queen Katherine away, Henry never saw her again. She was not allowed to see their only child, Princess Mary, who was kept at court with her father.

On September 7, 1533, Anne gave birth to their first child. It was a girl, whom they named Elizabeth. Henry sent a note to Katherine, demanding that she send the robes used for Mary's christening, but Katherine refused. When Katherine died in 1536, she wrote in her will that she still loved Henry and that she forgave him for everything. She also asked him to be good to their little daughter, Mary.

If Henry had waited three more years until Katherine died, he would have been free to marry Anne without making an enemy of Emperor

Charles or the pope. But the pope's sentence of excommunication from the Catholic Church—making him a kind of religious outlaw and releasing all his subjects from their duty of obeying him as their king—forced Henry to take extreme measures. What had begun as an obscure argument between church lawyers over a marriage annulment was to end as a religious revolution that would shake medieval Europe—especially England—like a massive earthquake.

A BEHEADING

When Henry married Anne Boleyn, he was forty-one, already an old man by the standards of the time. He was becoming desperate for a legal son and heir who would be king after him. This anxiety would ultimately lead him to marry four more times over the next ten years.

His marriage to Anne Boleyn did not last long. By 1536, her enemies had accused her of having sexual relations with other men at court and of using witchcraft to make Henry do whatever she wanted. The evidence against her was not strong, but Henry apparently believed it. Confessions were extracted from her alleged lovers under torture, and Anne was

This is an oil-on-wood painting of Jane Seymour, the mother of Edward VI. It was painted by Hans Holbein in 1536, one year before her death.

beheaded for betraying the trust of the king. For a married woman to have sexual relations with other men and to use witchcraft against her husband was known as petty treason. And if her husband was the king, it was a form of high treason.

Anne protested her innocence to the end. Some whispered that Henry had had her executed because she could not give him the son he wanted. She had several miscarriages and bore him only one healthy child—the future Queen Elizabeth I.

ANOTHER MARRIAGE

Royal marriages were not just for children. They were political and financial alliances. Every faction at court led by a rich and powerful family wanted Henry to marry one of their female relatives. When Henry showed that he would divorce or execute a queen and remarry as he pleased, the rivalry became bitter. The day after Anne's execution, Henry announced his plans to marry Jane Seymour.

The Princess Elizabeth was declared to be the child of one of Anne Boleyn's lovers. It was said that Elizabeth and Mary were not Henry's legal heirs. This way, Henry's illegitimate son, Henry Fitzroy, was next in line for the throne. Henry was extremely upset when the boy died two months later. However, his hopes rose when in the fall of 1537, Queen Jane gave birth to a baby boy, Prince Edward. He was crushed once again when twelve days after giving birth, the queen died of a fever. The impressive funeral Henry ordered for Jane was on a scale not seen since the funeral for his mother, Elizabeth of York, who had died thirty-five years earlier.

ROME, REFORMATION, AND REBELLION

In western Europe at this time, there was only one official church. The Catholic Church ruled from Rome by its elected chief bishop, the pope. But over the previous two centuries, increasing numbers of Christian groups criticized the beliefs and practices of the Catholic Church. The Catholic Church called these groups heretics. Heresy was a terrible crime, punishable by being burned alive, but this did not stop the tide of opposition. Church leaders and kings worried that the tide would one day become a flood.

In the sixteenth century, these heretics became known as Protestants because they protested against things that the Catholic Church said and did that seemed to contradict the teachings of Jesus as written in the Bible. Protestantism was strongest in Germany, and its most famous leader was a monk named Martin Luther. At first, the Protestants did not want to set up a church of their own in opposition to the Catholic Church. Instead, they simply wanted to reform it.

Moderates, like Erasmus and More (and Henry himself), also believed that the church needed reform. But when the pope threatened extreme critics like Luther with excommunication, Luther felt forced to break with Rome, while the moderates did not. Some

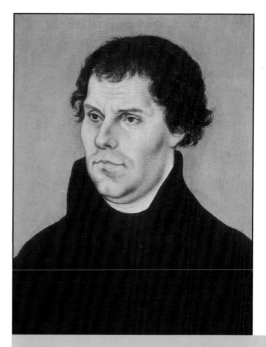

This 1526 painting shows Martin Luther. It was painted by Lucas Cranach the Elder. Martin Luther was a German monk who challenged the authority of the Catholic Church and began a movement that divided Europe. Henry VIII, who disliked what he had heard and read about Luther, was vocal about his point of view.

rulers supported Luther, for a variety of reasons.

DEFENDER OF THE FAITH

In 1521, Henry published a book defending the Catholic Church. The pope was delighted with it, and in recognition of Henry's championing the church against the Protestants, the pope gave Henry the official title *fidei defensor*, Latin for "the defender of the faith."

The Catholic conservatives said that if people were allowed to believe and behave as they liked, Christian civilization would collapse and Europe would soon be back in the Dark Ages. And if, as the Protestants demanded, all people were allowed free access to the Bible and church services in their own language, their ignorance would soon allow the devil to lead them astray.

However, by 1533, Henry himself had learned what it was like to be outlawed by the pope for following his conscience and doing what he believed to be right. Henry was still a Catholic, not a Protestant, even though, like Luther, he had been excommunicated. He decided that the church was still right, only that the pope was wrong. He felt that no pope should have the power to command obedience, since that was the right of kings.

Henry made himself the head of the Catholic Church in England. He ordered that all English clergy were answerable to him. He still kept the title of fidei defensor because now he felt he was defending the true faith of the church against the pope. And to this day, the kings and queens of England are still the heads of the Church of England, while every British coin bears an inscription calling the monarch fidei defensor.

With Wolsey disgraced and dead, Henry found a very efficient chief secretary named Thomas Cromwell to help More. Like Wolsey, Cromwell was a commoner who had risen high in the government service through talent and hard work. However, unlike More, Cromwell had strong Protestant sympathies and hated the power of the clergy. His first job was to draft new laws making the king head of the English church. One law levied a charge of treason on anyone who spoke against Henry's second marriage or criticized the king and his new queen. Another law made every government official swear an oath of allegiance to the king, Queen Anne, and their heirs.

OFF WITH YOUR HEAD

Cromwell organized a network of spies and informers. Anyone accused of having spoken against the king or Queen Anne, or defending Queen Katherine was likely to face arrest and interrogation at the very least. Many people began to be afraid and thought their king was becoming a tyrant. Some, like Bishop

This 1591 painting by Antoine Caron is entitled *The Arrest and Execution of Thomas More*. Caron lived from around 1515 to 1593. Sir Thomas More (1478– 1535) was trained as a lawyer and was distinguished as a scholar, statesman, and churchman. He was the author of *Utopia*, an account of an imaginary idealized society. He became Henry's chancellor and was executed on a charge of treason for refusing to swear to the Act of Supremacy. This act made the English monarch the head of the Church of England. More was beheaded in public.

John Fisher of Rochester, who had been an adviser of Henry's since he was a boy, refused to swear allegiance. Fisher was greatly respected for his knowledge, his piety, and his kindness, but this did not save him. He had written to Queen Katherine's nephew, the Emperor Charles V, urging him to invade England and restore the authority of the pope, the Catholic Church, and Queen Katherine's rights. But even if he had not done this, his refusal to swear allegiance would have been enough to convict him of treason. The penalty for treason was death. His head was cut off and displayed on London Bridge.

Only days later, in July 1535, Sir Thomas More suffered the same fate, simply for refusing to swear allegiance. Henry felt that he had to be firm and make no exceptions, even for a friend. These executions seemed to have the effect he wanted. If the king was prepared to execute old friends and members of the government, ordinary people knew that he would not tolerate opposition from anyone.

THE CHURCH'S WEALTH IS THE KING'S

At this time, Henry was badly in need of money. His extravagant lifestyle—building several new palaces, waging wars, his long lawsuit with Rome—had cost millions. And the threat of war was looming once more. The pope called all Catholic rulers to join in a crusade against England to depose Henry. It was certain that England's ancient enemies, France and Scotland, would attack sooner or later. Henry needed millions to build warships and castles for England's defense. While the expenses of government were rising rapidly, the royal income was not.

In 1536, Henry ordered Cromwell to make a thorough survey of the hundreds of monasteries and nunneries in the kingdom. The survey recorded how much each was worth in terms of land, property, and income. It also noted how many monks or nuns lived in each and whether or not they were well run. Cromwell's men were so efficient that the survey was completed in only six months.

Then, beginning with the smaller, poorly run monasteries, the king ordered that they be closed. Everything the monasteries owned became property of the Crown. Mostly, the buildings were demolished and the building materials, together with the monastery's valuables and land, were either auctioned or given by Henry to his New Men as a reward for good service. New Men, such as Cromwell, were people whom Henry had promoted to a high rank as

This photo shows the remains of Roche Abbey in Yorkshire. This is one of more than 800 monasteries that Henry closed. It was built by an order of monks called the Cistercians. They were named after their headquarters at Citeaux in France. They founded monasteries across Europe, including many in Britain. These were often in isolated, wild areas. The Cistercians were successful farmers and had become very rich by Henry's time. Henry dissolved all the monasteries in order to possess their wealth and lands.

a reward for their good service. Many aristocratic families who became powerful in Henry's time acquired their country mansions and estates in this way. Generations later, some of these families still own their estates.

The profit that Henry made from the monasteries was estimated at around 1.3 million pounds. This amount is hard to assess in modern terms. An ordinary person in England at the time would normally earn no more than five or six pounds in a year. Henry had enough money to pay his debts and wage war against the pope's allies.

THREAT OF CIVIL WAR

There was violent opposition to the destruction of the monasteries. A rebellion broke out in the northern counties, where there were numerous large monasteries that many working people depended on. They were supported by conservative aristocrats. These were Catholics who were loyal to the traditions of the old order. They hated to see the monasteries their families had endowed for centuries snapped up by the New Men who rivaled their aristocratic lifestyle. Thirty thousand rebels captured York, England's second most important city. Royal castles were seized, and Cromwell's agents were rounded up and killed.

Though Henry didn't have an army that was large enough to defeat the rebels, he needed to find a way to stop them. He sent the Duke of Norfolk—a conservative whom the rebels would trust and respect—to pretend to negotiate with them. The duke promised that the king would consider their demands and would give them a free pardon if they left. They obeyed and went home, believing that Henry would now do as they wished.

Months later, when the rebels saw that nothing had changed, they marched again. This time, the king's army was ready. The Duke of Norfolk was in command, and he had orders to show the rebels no mercy. Hundreds were hanged. Their bodies were left on gallows (devices used for hanging) beside the highways to remind everyone what happened to those who disobeyed.

By 1540, only four years later, every single monastery was closed. A way of life that had existed in England for centuries suddenly came to an end. While some of the monasteries had been harsh land-lords, many had been founded to provide education, health care, and relief for the poor. Their loss was deeply felt.

REFORMATION AWAY FROM ROME

Cromwell made other changes, in line with Protestant thinking. An official English translation of the Bible was published in 1537, and every church was ordered to buy one. Henry's new church was still Catholic in every respect except that it did not recognize the authority of the pope. Clergy were still not allowed to marry, and church services were still held in Latin. The old laws against heresy were strictly enforced as before, and many of the more radical Protestants escaped to Germany and Switzerland for safety. Henry was playing a dangerous game. This made him enemies among both Catholic nations that still obeyed the pope and countries that wholeheartedly followed the new Protestant faith. England and Henry stood alone on the brink of a religious war.

OLD KING HENRY

CHAPTER 7

Now in his mid-forties, Henry felt as though old age was creeping up on him. He had not jousted since 1536, when he had fallen and his horse landed on top of him. He had been unconscious for two hours, and the impact of the fall was so severe, many thought he had been killed. Though he survived, he was increasingly troubled by a sore on one leg that had not healed properly. Eventually, the infection spread to both legs and caused him great pain. Then, in 1538, he almost died—probably from a stroke. For twelve days, he was barely able to breathe and could not speak.

Meanwhile, some conservative factions at court (such as the Howards) were ready to support Princess Mary as queen if Henry were to die. Those with Protestant sympathies looked to the young Prince Edward and his

Seymour relatives. The country was on the verge of civil war.

ANOTHER MARRIAGE AND MORE BEHEADINGS

When Henry recovered from his illness, he felt he needed to marry again to have more sons to secure the succession. On Cromwell's advice, he made an alliance with the rich German Protestant

This portrait of Henry at age fifty-one is believed to have been painted by Hans Holbein. For this portrait, Holbein painted on wood with oil paint. Visible in this portrait is the fact that in his later years Henry had put on a lot of weight.

Duchy of Cleves. He agreed to marry the duke's daughter, Anne. For Cromwell, this was a double success. He had arranged a Protestant alliance and safely prevented any relative of the noble families who hated him from becoming queen. The aristocrats hated Cromwell, just as they had Wolsey. They resented his power and wealth and the influence he had on the king. To them, Cromwell was

73

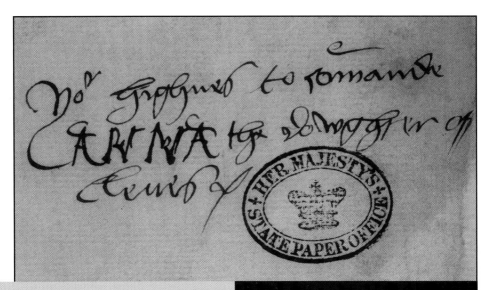

This portrait of Anne of Cleves *(right)* was painted by Hans Holbein from 1539 to 1540. Anne of Cleves (whose signature is shown above) was the daughter of Duke John of Cleves. The painting hangs in the Musée du Louvre in Paris. The painting was meant to be very flattering to Anne, who was not known for her good looks.

just another commoner who did not know his place.

Anne was twenty-four and well bred. Though lacking the socially important skills of music and dancing, she was intelligent and well enough educated to make a good companion for the king. As long as she obeyed him, could bear him male children, and did not object to his affairs with the other ladies at court (which was normal behavior for a king in those times), Henry would be satisfied.

By Christmas 1539, when Anne of Cleves came to England, she and Henry had still not even seen each other. However, they had both received flattering reports and pictures of each other from envoys eager to make the match. Anne's journey from Dover to London, with her retinue of 350 on snowbound roads, was slow. By New Year's Day 1540, Henry was so impatient to see her that he rode from London to Rochester, where her party had stopped. At Rochester, he walked in on her unannounced.

It was not a pleasant surprise for either of them. Old, balding, gray-bearded, and overweight at age forty-nine, Henry was not the well-built, handsome man that he had once been and that his portraits still showed him to be. Anne looked plain and dumpy to Henry. After the meeting, he referred to her as a "fat Flanders mare" (Flanders was famous for its huge draft horses). Her face was also pitted with scars from the smallpox she had suffered as a child. Henry was furious with his courtiers who had misinformed him—especially Cromwell. As soon as he had reluctantly escorted his unattractive bride-to-be back to London, he summoned Cromwell and told him to find a legal loophole for canceling the marriage.

Otherwise, Cromwell would lose his job. Henry decided that instead of marrying Anne, he would wed Catherine Howard, the pretty young niece of the Duke of Norfolk.

Cromwell knew that only the king's favor kept him from being at the mercy of the conservatives at court. Like Wolsey before him, he now had to deal with the task of canceling a marriage he had arranged for the king in order to make way for a new queen whose family wanted to destroy him. Unfortunately for Cromwell, he could find no legal reason for stopping the marriage. Because of this, Henry reluctantly married her.

That same year, Cromwell was accused of heresy and was beheaded without a trial. Henry had the marriage to Anne annulled on the grounds that he found her so unattractive he could not bring himself to have sex with her. As with Katherine of Aragon's marriage to Arthur, any marriage in which the partners had not had sexual relations was said to be invalid.

Anne swallowed her pride and accepted the judgment, together with a large pension and two royal manors near London. She continued to live in England and sometimes came to court, as she and Henry stayed on reasonably friendly terms. Perhaps she was grateful to have escaped the dangers of

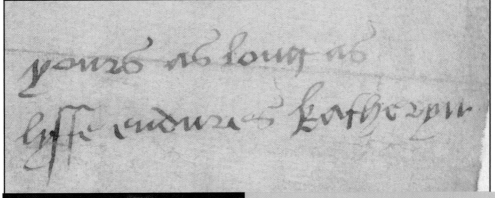

In this portrait, Catherine Howard, the fifth queen of King Henry VIII (whose signature is shown above), was painted in the style of Hans Holbein in the sixteenth century.

court politics with more than her life.

Henry and Catherine Howard were married on the same day Cromwell was executed. By 1541, Catherine had still not produced a child. Word then came to Henry from spies and enemies of the Howards that Catherine had lived a very immoral life before their marriage. Astonished and enraged, Henry put her under house arrest, dismissed her servants, and took away her possessions and even her title of queen. Further inquiries revealed that Catherine had also been unfaithful to Henry during their marriage. Catherine and her lovers were beheaded.

A FINAL BATTLE

Now that Henry was the pope's enemy, the new kings Francis I of France and James V of Scotland were eager to avenge the defeats their countries had suffered in 1513. They planned to invade England with the church's backing. Henry, remembering what had happened last time, decided to make sure of Scotland before risking another war in France.

A force of 18,000 Scots was moving south. James was ill and could not lead them, and his commanders argued over who should take charge. The English army, under Lord Hertford, took advantage of the confusion in the Scottish army and took 200 Scottish nobles prisoner. They captured thirty standards and twenty cannons. James V died a few days later, at the young age of twenty-nine. He left behind as his heir a day-old baby daughter who would later become Mary, Queen of Scots.

This is the armor of Archduke Maximilian, who later became the Holy Roman Emperor Maximilian I. This example of fifteenth-century armor is similar to what Henry and his soldiers would have worn in battle. Horses were also dressed in armor, both for protection and for pageantry. Horses were expensive and needed a fair amount of protection to carry a heavily armed rider.

Henry then sailed for France with his army, the Duke of Norfolk, and his old friend Charles Brandon. Brandon, who was now Duke of Suffolk, was in command. Henry captured the important French seaport of Boulogne. He left most of his soldiers to defend it and went home. It was the last time he would lead an army.

In 1545, King Francis counterattacked with a large fleet to destroy the English navy and land a French army in England. Another smaller French force was sent to land in Scotland and support another invasion by the Scottish lords. Meanwhile, a third French army tried to recapture Boulogne. It could have been a disaster for Henry, but the French forces, who were suffering from sickness and a shortage of supplies, gave up the invasion and returned home. The war achieved very little. However, Henry called it a victory because the French had not succeeded in invading or retaking Boulogne. It had cost Henry nearly two million pounds. His last chance to rival his ancestor Henry V and be crowned king of France had failed.

NEVER TOO OLD TO MARRY

Henry hated the fact that his fifth queen, Catherine Howard—a girl young enough to be his granddaughter—had made him look like an old fool. To him, it was perfectly acceptable for the king to seduce the ladies at court, but it was unforgivable for his queen to take lovers. His enormous pride was deeply hurt, and this made Henry angry with everyone.

He aged rapidly, and his gray hair turned white. He grew so obese through consoling himself with feasting that he had to be carried from room to room in a sedan chair. He avoided climbing stairs, living only on the ground floor.

This is a portrait of King Henry VIII's son, Edward VI, the Prince of Wales, at age five. Hans Holbein painted this portrait in 1542. In his arms, Edward is holding a long-tailed African monkey, called a guenon. The monkey was probably his pet, though it also signifies wealth and exotic taste. Edward would eventually become king of England from 1547 to 1553.

Henry, who had become an invalid, realized that he could not expect to live very much longer. To make matters worse, in the spring of 1542, the physicians of the royal household cautioned Henry that his son, Prince Edward VI, who was only four years old, was in poor health and would not likely live long. Henry's councillors advised him to marry once more and try again for another son and heir.

Understandably, there were not many women who could be persuaded to be Henry's queen. But by the following year, a suitable bride had been found. Catherine Parr had already been married twice, but

This is a portrait of Catherine Parr dated 1545. It is thought that the artist is Master John. Catherine was the sixth and last wife of King Henry VIII. After Henry died, she married Sir Thomas Seymour, Baron Seymour of Sudeley.

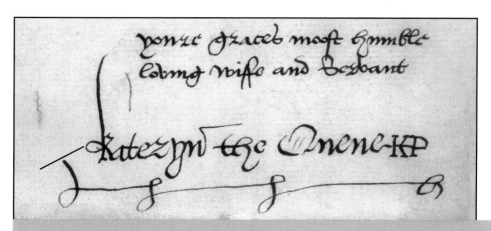

This is Catherine Parr's signature.

at thirty-one she was still young enough to have more children. She had been about to marry a courtier, but when Henry's councillors approached her with an offer of royal marriage, she seemed convinced that it was God's will that she should marry Henry. She hoped to use her influence to soothe his anger, which made him so dangerous.

She proved a kind mother to Henry's three children by his three previous wives—Mary, Katherine of Aragon's daughter, now twenty-six; Elizabeth, Anne Boleyn's daughter, age fourteen; and four-year-old Edward, Henry's son by Jane Seymour. She was as deeply religious as Henry but more radical. She urged Henry to make the church in England more Protestant than Catholic.

On one such occasion, Henry lost his temper with her, swearing that a man of his age and learning was not going to be taught religion by his wife. Catherine apologized. However, the next day, while she and Henry were walking in the gardens of Whitehall Palace, the Earl of Southampton came with soldiers to arrest her. Henry flew into a rage and drove the earl away, screaming curses at him. The day before, after their argument, Henry had decided to have Catherine arrested and imprisoned in the Tower of London on a charge of heresy. But after she apologized, he forgave her—only he had forgotten to cancel the order.

THE LAST DAYS

Henry was becoming more and more unpredictable. In 1546, he ordered the arrest of his most faithful supporter, the Duke of Norfolk, along with the duke's son, the young Earl of Surrey. He charged them with treason. The Protestant Seymours, who were allied with Catherine, now dominated the king's council and felt that they were strong enough to destroy their old enemies the Howards.

As Henry's health continued to decline, Edward Seymour, Lord Hertford, took control of the government. He used a stamp of the king's signature to authorize official documents. That winter, Henry became dangerously sick with a fever. Cooped up at Whitehall, with very few attendants, he spent his last Christmas alone—not even his family was allowed to come near him.

Henry gradually grew weaker until he could neither move nor speak. It's possible that he had suffered another stroke. On January 28, 1547, Henry died. His slow decline into unconsciousness was a stark contrast to the dynamic, golden-haired giant everyone remembered. His time had finally run out.

THE LEGACY

Henry's death was kept secret from everyone but the family for two days. Anyone asking to see the king was told he was too ill or too busy. As if nothing had happened, his huge meals continued to be prepared and were brought into the banquet hall accompanied by a fanfare of trumpets. It was not until January 30 that his death was made public.

Henry's will, though not officially signed by him, bore the impression of his signature since it had been "signed" with the stamp acquired by Lord Hertford. The will gave orders for a council of sixteen ministers (headed by Lord Hertford) to govern in the name of the new king, Edward VI, who was only nine years old. It is quite possible that Lord Hertford altered Henry's original will and forged a new copy.

The rest of the will gave instructions for burial in Windsor Castle, beside his third queen, Jane, mother of Edward. Since Lord Hertford was Jane's brother, he may also have added this to the will. Certain sums of money—large, but not really generous for a king— were to be given to the poor. Henry's personal servants and household officials were remembered in his will with gifts that corresponded to their rank. Queen Catherine received 4,000 pounds in money, gold, silver, and jewels. She also received a pension of 7,000 pounds a year, mostly from lands Henry had previously given to Anne Boleyn and Catherine Howard. This land had returned to Henry when they were executed for treason.

News traveled slowly on the wintry roads of sixteenth-century England, but by February 8, 1547, there was hardly anyone who did not know that old King Henry was dead. By order of the new king's council, all the church bells in the kingdom were rung in mourning, and special masses were said for his soul. Everyone—great aristocrats and simple peasants alike—must have had mixed feelings of relief and regret. However, the really important legacy was what Henry bequeathed to England and its people. Never in the history of England had so many momentous changes been brought about by a single ruler.

Pictured in this 1544 painting by an unknown artist are King Henry VIII, Jane Seymour, Prince Edward VI, and the Princesses Mary and Elizabeth. This is an important painting for two reasons. First, it is the earliest surviving group painting featuring Elizabeth. Also, the fact that the painting shows Mary and Elizabeth—whose mothers had been respectively divorced and executed by Henry—indicates that Henry acknowledged them as his legitimate children and therefore part of the succession for the monarchy. In the spring of 1544, Parliament formally restored Mary and Elizabeth to the succession. Jane Seymour was not alive at this date, but her importance to Henry as the mother of his male heir is emphasized. She was the only one of his wives for whom he wore mourning clothes. From right to left are Jane Bold, Mary, Edward, Henry, Jane Seymour, Elizabeth I, and Will Somers. Jane Bold was Princess Mary's fool, or jester. Will Somers was Henry's jester.

POLITICAL AND RELIGIOUS STRIFE

At the beginning of Henry's reign, the twenty-five-year civil war was a recent memory. England had been torn by conflict between two aristocratic factions.

These had formed because Henry V had died and left behind a young heir who was surrounded by powerful nobles who were greedy for wealth and power. By the end of Henry VIII's reign, despite all his efforts to prevent it, precisely the same thing had happened. And because of his break with Rome, the division between the court factions was not only personal and political, but religious, too. It was between the Catholics and the Protestants.

Henry helped make England a great nation, but many suffered as a result. Though he had become a tyrant, under his rule, England was secure, prosperous, and mainly peaceful. There was better law and order than anyone had known for a century, but much less freedom as well. And often, this is the price of a strong government. Now that he was dead, what would happen next? Who would take the enormous power the old king had gathered into his hands? Would a conservative or a radical group get the upper hand? Would England become Protestant, return to the Catholic Church, or keep a middle

This painting of Princess Elizabeth (dated around 1546) is the earliest surviving individual portrait of the teenage princess. The artist shows Elizabeth holding a book. The effect is almost as if the painter had interrupted her while she was reading and she is using her hand to keep her place in the text. There is another open book on the book stand beside her. Elizabeth was famous for (and proud of) her learning and intellect. She received an outstandingly good education. In this portrait, she is richly and fashionably dressed, reflecting her status as a king's daughter. She is shown wearing what was known as a French hood, which revealed and flattered the face.

course as it had under Henry? The answer would be all three, though this would be over the next ten years. There would be Protestantism under Edward VI and Lady Jane Grey, a return to Rome and Catholicism under Mary, then a middle course once more under Elizabeth. The tide of religious persecution, family feuds, and court politics would sweep from one extreme to the other.

HENRY'S STRENGTHS AND WEAKNESSES AS A KING

Henry made sure the nobles were kept in

check. He played them against each other and kept them at court where he could see them. If they misbehaved, he would order them put in prison under sentence of death. This also served as a warning to others. No one group was allowed to grow too powerful, except at the end, when, old and ailing, Henry could no longer stop the Seymours from becoming dominant.

Henry had also created an administration whose officials would keep the day-to-day business of government running smoothly no matter what happened. He was careful to keep clever, efficient officials in his service. No matter how humble their origin, he promoted them from his household to the highest rank in the council. He was also ruthless enough to get rid of them when they no longer served his purposes.

Henry's cruelty also extended to his wives and personal friends. Anyone who opposed him, no matter who they were, had to die. Everyone was his subject. And though they might disagree with Henry, it was their duty to obey him or risk death on a charge of treason.

Henry genuinely seemed to believe that what was good for the king was good for England. His conviction that he was always right fueled his will to succeed. It is easy to condemn him for his selfishness

Above: The *Mary Rose*, originally built by Henry the VIII in 1511. Left: This is a gold half-sovereign with an image of King Henry VIII sitting on his throne and wearing a crown. From its introduction in 1489 by Henry VII until 1526, the sovereign was valued at twenty shillings or one pound sterling. A shilling is one-twentieth of a pound, or from one to two days' wages for an unskilled laborer at the time. Similar coins were minted throughout Henry's reign.

and harshness, but it is hard to imagine what it is like for one person to have so much power. If he could not withstand the temptation to become a tyrant, perhaps it is not really surprising.

Henry made England into a center of learning and of arts and sciences. He built many fine palaces that were the talk of Europe. He gave England a modern, well-equipped navy that would one day come to dominate the world. He made England safe from invasion with a ring of strong fortresses, and he modernized the army. He never lost a war, and although his military spending nearly bankrupted the treasury, every foreign neighbor looked on Henry's England with a new respect.

It was under Henry that the English Bible first became widely available. Henry said it was intended to help the people understand the teachings of the Catholic Church (as understood by Henry), not to help them make up their own minds about religion. However, that is exactly what happened. In this way,

Henry was directly responsible for the conflict of ideas that would engulf England a century later. This ended with the execution of one king and the exile of another. England would first become a republic, then a compromise of democracy and monarchy. Henry VIII began these changes, and they are part of his legacy.

TIMELINE

1491	Prince Henry Tudor is born at Greenwich Palace.
1503	Prince Arthur dies. Henry becomes Prince of Wales.
1509	Henry VII dies. Henry VIII becomes king at age seventeen. Henry marries Katherine of Aragon.
1513	England is at war with France and Scotland.
1515	King Henry VIII builds a great tournament ground at Greenwich.
1516	Mary I (1516–1558) is born at Greenwich Palace.
1530	Cardinal Wolsey dies.
1533	Henry marries Anne Boleyn in secret. Elizabeth I (1533–1603) is born at Greenwich Palace.
1534	The Act of Supremacy is put into effect, thus making Henry head of the Church of England.
1535	Sir Thomas More and Bishop Fisher are executed for treason.
1536	Katherine of Aragon dies. Anne Boleyn is executed for treason. Henry marries Jane Seymour. There is a union with Wales.
1537	Edward VI, Henry's son, is born. Jane Seymour dies.
1540	All monasteries are closed under Henry's orders. Henry marries Anne of Cleves. The marriage is annulled six months later. Thomas Cromwell is executed for heresy. Henry marries Catherine Howard.
1542	Catherine Howard is executed for treason.
1543	Henry marries Catherine Parr.
1545	England goes to war with France.
1547	Edward VI (1537–1553) becomes king of England on the death of Henry VIII.

GLOSSARY

abbey A large, important monastery or nunnery. Smaller establishments were known as priories.

alchemy The forerunner of chemistry, based on the belief that one substance can be turned into another by a variety of treatments. The main interest in alchemy was the attempt to make gold out of cheaper metals.

ancestry Aristocratic families in Europe reckoned their descent from royal ancestors. The more closely related an aristocrat was to a king or a queen, the stronger his or her claim to rule a country.

annulment Canceling a contract, such as marriage, usually on the grounds that the contract was never legally valid. In the sixteenth century, it was easier to get a marriage annulled than to get a divorce. A divorce could only be granted if either the husband or the wife's behavior was unacceptable in the Catholic Church.

Aragon The former province of northeast Spain, originally a separate kingdom.

archbishop A senior bishop, with authority over all the other bishops in a particular area. In England, there were two archbishops: one in Canterbury and the other in York. The archbishop of Canterbury was senior to the archbishop of York.

cardinal A senior priest in the Catholic Church, usually a bishop, who often represents the pope when he is away from Rome. When a pope dies, the cardinals meet and elect one of their number to be the new pope.

Chapel Royal Like the court, not a fixed place or a building, but a body of people consisting of musicians, clergy, and choristers (singers) who provided religious services for the king.

chaplain A priest employed by an aristocratic family to look after that family's spiritual needs, usually out of a private chapel.

chivalric Following the code of chivalry, an informal set of traditional moral guidelines developed in the early Middle Ages for the behavior of knights.

christening Literally, "making Christian." The rite of baptism.

Cinque Ports Five ports on the coast of England nearest France (from the Old French word *cinque*, meaning "five"). In return for certain privileges, these five ports had to supply men and ships to the king in time of war.

commoner Anyone who was not a knight, a lady, or a member of the titled aristocracy. The term can also be used to refer to anyone who is not a member of a royal family.

constable A military governor who answers directly to the king. Every royal castle had a constable, and there was also a constable of England who would direct the country's defense if the king was ill or abroad.

coronation The ceremony of making a new king or queen, especially the part in which the crown is placed on the head of the king or queen for the first time. The ceremony is performed by the country's most senior bishops.

Dark Ages The period between the fall of the Roman Empire in the fourth century and the emergence of the modern states of western Europe in the eighth century, from which time the Middle Ages are generally believed to have begun. The Dark Ages are traditionally thought of as a time when civilization in western Europe collapsed.

dominion Territory abroad owned by the king, usually acquired by inheritance, by marriage, or by conquest. The kings of England had rights to lands in France based on all three.

dowry Property customarily given by a bride's father when she is married. It could take the form of money, valuables, or land. After marriage, it became the property of her husband, but if he died and left her a widow, the dowry was to returned to her. Medieval marriages were usually not love matches but business transactions.

duke The highest rank in the titled aristocracy. The children of kings and queens of England are also often dukes or duchesses. This is also the highest rank a commoner can attain without becoming part of the royal family.

earl A middle-ranking nobleman, higher than a viscount or baron but lower than a marquis or duke.

Flanders Part of modern Belgium, Holland, and Germany, also known in the sixteenth century as the Low Country because it lay very close to sea level.

heresy A controversial opinion.

jester Also known as a fool, a professional comedian who is employed in a royal or noble household. Jesters were often very wise, as they had to understand all sorts of people very well to be able to make them laugh.

jousting A popular martial art in the Middle Ages, in which pairs of armored horsemen would charge at each other and try to knock their opponent off of his horse. Also known as tilting.

Lancastrian A member of a group supporting the claim to rule England of aristocrats descended from Edward III's third son, John, Duke of Lancaster.

longbow A bow made from yew wood and nearly as tall as the person it was made for. Twice the size of bows in normal use elsewhere in Europe, it was a standard English infantry weapon. The longbow was known for its power, accuracy, and range. An archer needed a great deal of training and strength to use it to its full effect. Longbows were also used for hunting.

lute A stringed instrument played like a guitar and very popular in Europe during the Middle Ages. Invented by the Arabs, it was brought back to Europe during the Crusades.

Mass The most important religious rite of the Catholic Church, in which consecrated bread and wine are believed to become the body and blood of Jesus. The Mass is also known as the Eucharist or Holy Communion.

matins A morning service in the Catholic Church, held before Mass.

Midsummer Day An important festival day in the Catholic calendar, commemorating the death of Saint John the Baptist (June 24). It was also regarded as the midpoint of summer in Europe.

minstrel A professional musician.

miser An obsessive hoarder of money, always eager to get more but very reluctant to spend any.

Such behavior was regarded by the Catholic Church
ght to be a kind of men-

ury term for the upwardly
dle class who were pro-
or service to the king.
the aristocracy had to be

it in aristocratic and royal
of aristocratic background.
dren to serve in the
, as part of their educa-
od servant knows how he

mployed by the monarch
royal occasions.

expert advisers appointed

nts and objects said to
elieved by Catholics to
wer of holiness. A relic's
is believed to help the
tact with it.

ervants and followers of

s of the Catholic Church by
directly invoked. There
are seven sacraments—baptism, first communion,
confirmation, penance (the forgiveness of sins),

ordination (initiation into the clergy), marriage, and unction (an anointing for the dangerously ill).

standard   Royal flags were known as standards and were a rallying point for the whole army, since they showed where the king was.

standard-bearer   Medieval aristocrats went into battle displaying flags with their personal emblems so they could easily be seen by their followers. A standard-bearer was a trusted soldier whose courage, loyalty, and fighting ability were outstanding. To lose a standard to the enemy was regarded as a deep disgrace. The standard-bearer was usually also a personal friend of the king.

tiltyard   A long enclosure in the grounds of a castle or palace designed for jousting.

vespers   An evening service of prayer in the Catholic Church, also known as evensong.

Westminster Abbey   The chief place of public worship and celebration of religious ceremonies for the royal family in London, especially for state occasions such as coronation. Although all the monks had left by 1540, the huge abbey church, which is as big as a cathedral, is still known as Westminster Abbey. Most of the kings and queens of England are buried there.

Whitehall   A former palace in London, owned by Cardinal Wolsey and taken from him by Henry VIII, who made it his chief London residence. It is now a complex of buildings that still forms the administrative center of the United Kingdom.

Yorkist A member of a faction supporting aristocrats descended from the fourth son of Edward III, Edmund, Duke of York, in their claim to the throne of England.

FOR MORE INFORMATION

WEB SITES
Due to the changing nature of Internet links, the Rosen Publishing Group, Inc., has developed an online list of Web sites related to the subject of this book. This site is updated regularly. Please use this link to access the list:

http://www.rosenlinks.com/lema/heei

FOR FURTHER READING

Chandler, John. *John Leland's Itinerary: Travels in Tudor England*. Dover, NH: Alan Sutton, 1993.

Fraser, Antonia. *The Six Wives of Henry VIII*. London: Wedenfeld & Nicolson, 1992.

Shakespeare, William. *The Famous History of the Life of King Henry the Eighth*. New York: New American Library, 1968.

BIBLIOGRAPHY

Bowle, John. *Henry VIII*. Boston: Brown, 1965.

Britnell, Richard. *The Closing of the Middle Ages: England, 1471–1529*. Oxford, England: Blackwell, 1997.

Bruce, Marie Louise. *The Making of Henry VIII*. Toronto, ON: Collins, 1977.

Englander, David, et al. *Culture and Belief in Europe, 1450–1600: An Anthology of Sources*. Cambridge, MA: Blackwell, 1990.

Erickson, Carolly. *Great Harry: A Life of King Henry VIII*. New York: St. Martin's Press, 1997.

Great Britain Department of the Environment. *Armours of Henry VIII*. London: Her Majesty's Stationery Office, 1977.

Lisle, Viscount, and Arthur Plantagenet. *The Lisle Letters*. Chicago: University of Chicago Press, 1981.

McDonald, Fiona. *You Wouldn't Want to Be Married to Henry VIII: A Husband You'd Rather Not Have*. London: Hodder Wayland, 2001.

Miller, Helen. *Henry VIII and the English Nobility.* New York: Blackwell, 1986.

Newcombe, D. G. *Henry VIII and the English Reformation.* New York: Routledge, 1995.

Pollard, A. F. *Henry VIII.* New York: Longmans, 1913.

Public Record Office of Great Britain. *Tudor Royal Letters: The Family of Henry VIII.* London: Her Majesty's Stationery Office, 1972.

Strong, Roy. *Holbein: The Complete Paintings.* New York: Granada, 1980.

Weir, Alison. *The Children of Henry VIII, 1547–1558.* New York: Ballantine Books, 1996.

Williams, Neville. *Henry VIII and His Court.* New York: Macmillan, 1971.

Wilson, Derek. *In the Lion's Court: Power, Ambition and Sudden Death in the Court of Henry VIII.* London: Hutchinson, 2001.

INDEX

ABOUT THE AUTHOR

Nick Ford studied comparative religion at the University of Lancaster and recently gained a first-class joint honors degree from the Open University in European humanities and classical studies. He is currently engaged in part-time postgraduate research at the University of Southampton. He has also worked for fifteen years as a costumed interpreter at a number of historical sites in Britain and has written papers on medieval and Roman history. He particularly enjoys studying the religion and everyday life of both periods. He lives in Southampton with his wife, Carol, and two cats, Ted and Rosie.

CREDITS

Editor: Annie Sommers
Designer: Evelyn Horovicz
Photo Researcher: Elizabeth Loving